How to Use a Dictionary
How to Use a Thesaurus

48 Fun Activities for Students

Learning Dictionary and Thesaurus Skills

Mary Wood Cornog, Ph.D and
The Editors of Merriam-Webster

FEDERAL
STREET
PRESS

A Division of Merriam-Webster, Incorporated
Springfield, Massachusetts

This 2006 edition published by
Federal Street Press
A Division of Merriam-Webster, Incorporated
P.O. Box 281
Springfield, MA 01102

Federal Street Press books are available for bulk purchase for sales promotion
and premium use. For details write the manager of special sales, Federal Street
Press, P.O. Box 281, Springfield, MA 01102

ISBN10 1-59695-013-7
ISBN13   978-1-59695-013-9

Text design by Joyce C. Weston

Printed in the United States of America

06 07 08 09 10   5 4 3 2 1

Contents

Preface

Open a dictionary to any page. What do you see? One thing you'll probably notice right away is that some words are printed in heavy **boldface** type. Other words are printed in all capital letters (like this: INSTANCE), and some parts of each dictionary entry are printed in slanted *italic* type. You'll see slash marks with strange characters between them (\ig-ˈzam-pəl\), funny dots in the middle of words (di·vi·sion), and sections of words marked off by pointed brackets, like these < >. You'll see numbers and colons (:). You'll see pictures.

This can all be a bit confusing, especially if you are new to using dictionaries. But don't worry. The purpose of this book is to make you familiar with these different parts of the dictionary. By the time you have finished the lessons, all the funny-looking characters and print types on the dictionary page will make sense to you, and you'll be able to use the dictionary as an effective tool in your schoolwork.

Thesauruses are similar to dictionaries in some ways and different in others. Thesauruses consist mostly of lists of words. You can use a thesaurus to find a word that fits a particular situation (though you should always check a good dictionary before using a word that is new to you). In the thesaurus section of this book, we'll talk about the features of a typical thesaurus entry so you will be familiar with them as well.

It can sometimes be frustrating to encounter words you don't know the meaning of, or to want to say something and not know the right words to use. When used effectively, dictionaries and thesauruses can remove frustration by increasing your knowledge. They are useful tools that can open up a world of meaning and help make you a better reader, writer, and speaker.

So let's get started!

Using This Book

This book consists of 26 lessons which are followed by an answer key.

Each lesson consists of explanatory text, illustrative examples from the dictionary or thesaurus, and exercises. The exercises are intended to reinforce the explanations. Students should read the text portion of each lesson carefully before doing the exercises.

This book aims to provide a thorough and comprehensive introduction to using a dictionary and thesaurus. If students, teachers, or parents have questions that have not been covered, however, they should consult the explanatory notes printed in the front of both the dictionary and thesaurus.

How to Use a
Dictionary

Alphabetical Order— Getting Started

Scan your eyes down the columns on your dictionary page and you'll see that each of the **dictionary entries** begins with a **boldface** word that sticks out into the margin just a little to catch the eye. This boldface word is called the **entry word** or **main entry**.

> **aback** \ə-'bak\ *adv* : by surprise <taken *aback* by the change in plan>
> **aba·cus** \'ab-ə-kəs\ *n, pl* **aba·ci** \'ab-ə-ˌsī\ or **aba·cus·es** : an instrument for doing arithmetic by sliding counters along rods or in grooves
> **abaft** \ə-'baft\ *adv* : toward or at the back part of a ship
> **ab·a·lo·ne** \ˌab-ə-'lō-nē\ *n* : a large sea snail that has a flattened shell with a pearly lining

One of the most important things to understand about a dictionary is that all of the main entries are arranged in **alpha-betical order**. We call this **alphabetization**. To use a dictionary effectively, you'll need to become very familiar with alphabetization. It can take some practice, but once you get good at it, you'll be able to locate the words you are looking for with ease.

The basic concept of alphabetical order is simple. Since *a* comes before *b* and *b* comes before *c* in the alphabet, all of the words beginning with *a* come before those that begin with *b*, the *b* words come before the *c* words, and so on all the way through the dictionary.

> **ab·sence** \'ab-səns\ *n* **1** : a being away...
> **bank·er** \'bang-kər\ *n* : a person who...
> **cal·li·ope** \kə-'lī-ə-pē\ *n* : a keyboard...
> **de·light·ful** \di-'līt-fəl\ *adj* : giving delight...
> **en·ter·tain** \ˌent-ər-'tān\ *vb* **1** : to greet...

Test Your Alphabet Skills

Put each series of words in the correct alphabetical order.

1. cat, mouse, dog, horse, pig

_____ _____ _____ _____ _____

2. sled, jaunt, lyric, umbrella, TV

_____ _____ _____ _____ _____

3. vitamin, acrobat, lazy, octopus, noodle

_____ _____ _____ _____ _____

Alphabetical order also applies within each group of words that share the same first letter. This means that all of the words with the same first letter are then sorted by their second letter.

> **ear·ring** \'ir-,ring\ *n* : an ornament worn...
> **ed·i·ble** \'ed-ə-bəl\ *adj* : fit or safe to eat
> **enig·ma** \i-'nig-mə\ *n* : something hard...

Test Your Alphabet Skills
Put each series of words in the correct alphabetical order.

1. bad, broccoli, bike, boy, blouse

_____ _____ _____ _____ _____

2. sunny, share, seven, snap, store

_____ _____ _____ _____ _____

3. ivy, industry, ignition, icy, irk

_____ _____ _____ _____ _____

Those words with the same first and second letters are then sorted according to their third letter. Words with the same first, second, and third letter are sorted according to their fourth letter, and so on.

> **fig** \'fig\ *n* : an edible fruit that is oblong...
> **fire·plug** \'fīr-,pləg\ *n* : HYDRANT
> **first·hand** \'fərst-'hand\ *adj* or *adv*...

Test Your Alphabet Skills
Put each series of words in the correct alphabetical order.

1. chop, chalk, chili, cheese, chute

_____ _____ _____ _____ _____

2. cannon, capstan, capacious, canopy, capable

_____ _____ _____ _____ _____

3. dragonfly, dragnet, dragoon, draggle, dragon

_____ _____ _____ _____ _____

Alphabetical Order— Moving Along

When words are arranged in alphabetical order, hyphens or spaces in the words don't count. You'll also want to ignore the **boldface** dots in the entry words when you are looking up words in the dictionary. (We'll explain what these dots are in lesson 4.) When you are trying to decide where a word with a hyphen, space, or boldface dot belongs in an alphabetized list, skip over that place in the word and look to the next letter in line.

Also, a word like **to** that has no letters after the second spot comes before a word like **toad**, with an **a** in the third spot. The entry **ill** comes before **illegal**, and so on.

> ³**high** *n* **1 :** the space overhead : SKY <watched the birds on *high*> **2 :** a region of high barometric pressure **3 :** a high point or level <prices reached a new *high*> **4 :** the arrangement of gears in an automobile giving the highest speed of travel
>
> **high·brow** \'hī-ˌbraů\ *n* : a person of great learning or culture
>
> **high fidelity** *n* : the reproduction of sound with a high degree of accuracy
>
> **long–lived** \'lȯng-'līvd, -'livd\ *adj* : living or lasting for a long time
>
> **long–range** \'lȯng-'rānj\ *adj* **1** : capable of traveling or shooting great distances **2** : lasting over or providing for a long period
>
> **long·sight·ed** \'lȯng-'sīt-əd\ *adj* : FAR-SIGHTED — **long·sight·ed·ness** *n*
>
> **long–suf·fer·ing** \'lȯng-'səf-ə-ring, -'səf-ring\ *adj* : very patient and forgiving

Test Your Alphabet Skills

Put each series of words in the correct alphabetical order.

1. fir, fire escape, fire·crack·er, figure out, figure of speech

_____ _____ _____ _____ _____

2. al·lude, any·wise, any, any·one, all-star

_____ _____ _____ _____ _____

3. double play, dou·ble, double bass, dou·ble·head·er, dou·ble-joint·ed

_____ _____ _____ _____ _____

4. man·i·fold, man, man-made, man·age·ment, man·age

_____ _____ _____ _____ _____

5. sign language, sig·nal, sign·post, sig·nif·i·cance, sign·board

_____ _____ _____ _____ _____

Amazing Results!

Find your way through the maze by proceeding from one word to the next in alphabetical order.

Start Here ↓

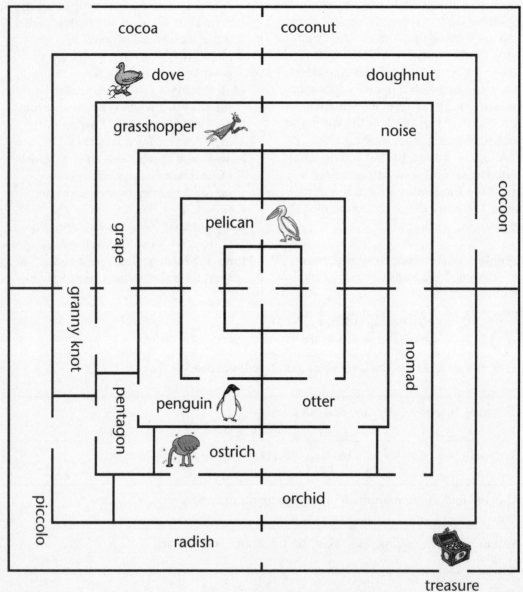

cocoa coconut

dove doughnut

grasshopper noise

cocoon

grape

pelican

granny knot

nomad

pentagon

penguin otter

ostrich

piccolo

orchid

radish

treasure

Guide Words

If you've learned alphabetization, you've already mastered the most important skill you need to find the words you are looking for in the dictionary. But the dictionary also has a special feature that can help you find words even faster. To save you from having to search up and down page after page looking for the word you want, most dictionaries print a pair of **guide words** at the top of each page. They are usually the alphabetically first and last entry on the page. By looking at the guide words and thinking about whether the word you are hunting for will fit alphabetically between them, you can quickly move from page to page to find the right one.

Say for example, you are looking up **gamma rays** and you have already turned to the section of words that begin with the letter **g**. You next should look at the guide words at the top of the pages. The exact guide words will vary from dictionary to dictionary, but you might, for example, see a page that has **gaff · gamekeeper** in its top corner, followed by a page with **gamely · garment**.

You know that **gamma rays** is alphabetically after **gamekeeper**, the last guide word on the first page, so you want to look beyond that page. On the next page, you see the guide words **gamely** and **garment**. You know that **gamma rays** comes after **gamely** and before **garment**, so this must be the page you want.

mountain goat
to mouse

Test Your Guide Word Skills

Use the guide word method to find the following words in your dictionary. Write the guide words in the spaces provided.

1. counterfeit   _____   _____

2. sculpture   _____   _____

3. offshore   _____   _____

4. messy   _____   _____

5. however   _____   _____

6. tangible   _____   _____

7. babble   _____   _____

8. gap   _____   _____

9. colt   _____   _____

10. collarbone   _____   _____

11. siesta   _____   _____

12. periscope   _____   _____

13. saga   _____   _____

14. barnyard   _____   _____

15. banquet   _____   _____

16. usable   _____   _____

17. humorous   _____   _____

18. hurtle   _____   _____

19. adobe   _____   _____

20. depth   _____   _____

End-of-Line Divisions

Most of the entry words in the dictionary are shown with dots at several places in the word. These dots are not part of the spelling of the word. They are only there to show **end-of-line division**—places where you can put a hyphen if you have to break a word into two pieces because there is not room for all of it at the end of a line.

Let's say you are writing a story for school and you have come to the end of the line on your page. You have started to write the word *armadillo* when you realize you don't have enough space left for the whole word. You can write part of the word on one line, ending with a hyphen, and put the rest of it on the following line. But you shouldn't just break the word anywhere. There's a right way and a wrong way to do it—and you can find the right way at the word's entry in the dictionary.

> **ar·ma·dil·lo** \ˌär-mə-ˈdil-ō\ *n, pl*
> **ar·ma·dil·los** : a small burrowing animal of Latin America and Texas whose head and body are protected by a hard bony armor

In this example, the dots show three different places where you can break the word and put a hyphen.

> | | |
> |---|---|
> | ar- | madillo |
> | arma- | dillo |
> | armadil- | lo |

Words should not be divided so that only one letter stays at the end of a line or comes at the beginning of the next line. This is the reason no dot is shown after the first letter of the word *abandon* or before the last letter of the word *banana*.

> **¹aban·don** \ə-ˈban-dən\ *vb*...
> **ba·nana** \bə-ˈnan-ə\ *n*...

When two or more main entries have the same spelling and the same end-of-line divisions, the dots indicating these divisions are shown only in the first of the entries.

> **¹mo·tion** \ˈmō-shən\ *n*...
> **²motion** *vb*...

You would divide the verb *motion* the same as the noun *motion*, but the dictionary shows the dots only once.

Segmenting Words

In the words below, put a dot at each place where the word can be divided at the end of a line. Use the dictionary to be sure you place the dots in the right spots.

1. e m p e r o r

2. s n o w m a n

3. c r a y o n

4. o x y g e n

5. p i z z a

6. m i s c o n d u c t

7. p a j a m a s

8. a s t e r o i d

9. t e d d y   b e a r

10. m a c a w

11. t e a c h e r

12. g l o b a l

13. z o d i a c

14. i m p e r s o n a l

15. p y r a m i d

16. p i c k e r e l

17. p l a t y p u s

18. o b e l i s k

19. b r o t h e r

20. r e l a t i o n s h i p

21. e d u c a t i o n

22. p o m e g r a n a t e

23. i m p o r t a n c e

24. r o y a l t y

25. o r i o l e

26. o r a n g u t a n

27. o c t a g o n

28. t o u r n a m e n t

29. m i s t l e t o e

30. k o a l a

31. c a r t o o n

32. s o u t h w e s t e r n

33. g l o c k e n s p i e l

34. c h e m i c a l

35. a t y p i c a l

36. s a n d p a p e r

Pronunciation

One thing you will certainly notice as you look at your dictionary page is the strange-looking symbols that appear between slanted lines.

\\ˈärd-ˌvärk\\ \\ˈdēp-ˈfrī\\ \\ˈhət\\ \\ˈtər-ˌmȯil\\

These are the **pronunciation symbols**.

Dictionaries use pronunciation symbols to help you learn how each word should sound. In most cases, you'll see a respelling of the word using pronunciation symbols directly after the **boldface** entry word.

sauce \\ˈsȯs\\ *n* **1 :** a tasty liquid poured over food **2 :** stewed fruit <cranberry *sauce*>
sauce·pan \\ˈsȯs-ˌpan\\ *n* : a small deep cooking pan with a handle
sau·cer \\ˈsȯ-sər\\ *n* : a small shallow dish often with a slightly lower center for holding a cup

Each pronunciation symbol stands for one important sound in English. To help you "decode" each sound, your dictionary has included special **pronunciation keys**. In the keys, the symbols are followed by words that contain the sound of each symbol.

ā... **da**y, f**a**de, m**a**te, v**a**c**a**tion

The boldface letters in the words show by example the sounds that the symbols represent. In other words, the key tells you that whenever you see the symbol ā, you should pronounce it the way you would pronounce the boldface vowel sounds in the words *day, fade, mate,* and *vacation.*

You'll find a large key at the beginning of the dictionary showing all of the symbols, and you'll find a smaller key showing some of the symbols at the bottom of the odd numbered pages of the book.

\\ə\\ **a**bout	\\au̇\\ **ou**t	\\i\\ t**i**p	\\ȯ\\ s**aw**
\\u̇\\ f**oo**t	\\ər\\ f**ur**th**er**	\\ch\\ **ch**in
\\ī\\ l**i**fe	\\ȯi\\ c**oi**n	\\y\\ **y**et	\\a\\ m**a**t
\\e\\ p**e**t	\\j\\ **j**ob	\\th\\ **th**in	\\yü\\ f**ew**
\\ā\\ t**a**ke	\\ē\\ **ea**sy	\\ng\\ si**ng**	\\t͟h\\ **th**is
\\yu̇\\ c**u**re	\\ä\\ c**o**t, c**ar**t	\\g\\ **g**o
\\ō\\ b**o**ne	\\ü\\ f**oo**d	\\zh\\ vi**si**on

Until you've learned the sound for each symbol, you should refer to the keys often as you sound out pronunciations in the dictionary.

What's That Sound?

Here are eight sets of pronunciations for eight words. For each word, there are three possibilities. Using the dictionary, find the correct pronunciation for each word and put a check next to it.

Note: We'll explain about the hyphens and the stress marks (which look like this ' or this ,) in the next lesson. You can ignore them for now.

1. hunch	___'hench	___'hunch	___'hənch
2. ecology	___u-'kal-a-jē	___i-'käl-ə-jē	___e-'kol-i-je
3. percussion	___pər-'kəsh-ən	___par-'kich-in	___por-'kich-ən
4. shamrock	___'shäm-ˌrok	___'sham-ˌrək	___'sham-ˌräk
5. zodiac	___'zod-e-ˌak	___'zōd-ē-ˌak	___'zud-e-ˌak
6. hibernate	___'hī-bər-ˌnāt	___'hi-ber-ˌnat	___'hə-bər-ˌnät
7. fiesta	___fi-'es-'tē	___fa-'es-te	___fē-'es-tə
8. useful	___'üs-ful	___'yus-fül	___'yüs-fəl

What's That Word?

Use the pronunciation keys in your dictionary to "decode" the pronunciations on the left. Draw a line connecting each pronunciation to the correct word on the right.

\'ap-əl\	hot dog
\im-ˌaj-ə-'nā-shən\	fun
\'hōm-ˌwərk\	onion
\'fan\	imagination
\'ən-yən\	fine
\'fin\	apple
\'jī-ənt\	south
\'hät-ˌdȯg\	fin
\'fən\	homework
\'saùth\	fan
\'fīn\	giant

More About Pronunciation

Many of the pronunciations in the dictionary are broken into smaller sections, called **syllables**. Merriam-Webster dictionaries use hyphens with the pronunciation symbols to show the syllables of a word, as in these examples.

> **beast** \'bēst\ *n*...
> (1 syllable)
> **bed·side** \'bed-ˌsīd\ *n*...
> (2 syllables)
> **east·er·ly** \'ē-stər-lē\ *adj* or *adv*...
> (3 syllables)
> **op·ti·mism** \'äp-tə-ˌmiz-əm\ *n*...
> (4 syllables)

Some syllables of a word are spoken with greater force, or **stress**, than others. Three kinds of stress are shown in Merriam-Webster dictionaries.

Primary stress, or **strong stress**, is shown by a high mark (like this ') placed before a syllable. The first syllable of **easterly** has a primary stress in our example. This means it gets spoken with a little extra force when you say the word. To see what we mean, try saying the word

easterly several times out loud putting the stress on a different syllable each time. It should sound a little strange to you when you put the emphasis on the second or third syllables.

Secondary stress, or **medium stress**, is shown by a low mark (like this ˌ) before a syllable. The second syllable in **bedside** and the third syllable in **optimism** have secondary stress. Secondary stress means the syllable is spoken with some force, but not as much as with primary stress.

The third kind of stress, **weak stress**, has no mark before syllables. These syllables are the ones that are spoken without much force at all.

Each of the three kinds of stress is shown in the pronunciation of **penmanship**.

> **pen·man·ship** \'pen-mən-ˌship\ *n*...

The first syllable has primary stress. The second syllable has weak stress. The third syllable has secondary stress. Say the word to yourself so you can hear each kind of stress.

beast

Find the Syllables

Look up the following words in your dictionary. Insert the missing hyphens in the correct spot of each pronunciation.

favorable \\'f ā v ə r ə b ə l\\

dinosaur \\'d ī n ə ,s ȯ r\\

runaway \\'r ə n ə ,w ā\\

outpatient \\'a u̇ t ,p ā s h ə n t\\

papaya \\p ə 'p ī ə\\

recorder \\r i 'k ȯ r d ə r\\

apologize \\ə 'p ä l ə ,j ī z\\

majesty \\'m a j ə s t ē\\

pacific \\p ə 's i f i k\\

television \\'t e l ə ,v i z h ə n\\

All Stressed Out

Here are some pronunciations that are missing their stress marks. Look up the words, then indicate **primary** and **secondary stress** for each pronunciation.

holiday \\ häl- ə- dā\\

magpie \\ mag- pī\\

toothbrush \\ tüth- brəsh\\

topsy-turvy \\ täp- sē- tər- vē\\

katydid \\ kāt- ē- did\\

foolhardy \\ fül- härd- ē\\

probability \\ präb- ə- bil- ət- ē\\

sedimentary \\ sed- ə- ment- ə- rē\\

wayside \\ wā- sīd\\

navigation \\ nav- ə- gā- shən\\

Putting It All Together

Look up the following words. Add the hyphens *and* the stress marks to the pronunciations.

navy \\ n ā v ē\\

teenager \\ t ē n ā j ə r\\

telepathy \\ t ə l e p ə t h ē\\

alumna \\ ə l ə m n ə\\

meteor \\ m ē t ē ə r\\

strawberry \\ s t r ȯ b e r ē\\

everyday \\ e v r ē d ā\\

luminous \\ l ü m ə n ə s\\

zodiac \\ z ō d ē a k\\

finale \\ f ə n a l ē\\

Still More About Pronunciation

Many words are pronounced in two, three, or even more different ways. Two or more pronunciations for a single entry are separated by commas, as in the following example.

> ¹**ra·tion** \'rash-ən, 'rā-shən\ *n*...

The order in which different pronunciations for the same word are given does not mean that the pronunciation given first is somehow better or more correct than the others. Both pronunciations of **ration** are equally acceptable, for example. You can choose the pronunciation that sounds most natural to you—you will be correct whichever one you use.

Sometimes when a second or third pronunciation is shown, only part of the pronunciation of the word changes. When this happens, the dictionary may show only the section that changes.

> **greasy** \'grē-sē, -zē\ *adj*...
> **pa·ja·mas** \pə-'jäm-əz, -'jam-əz\ *n pl*...

To get the full second or third pronunciation of a word, add the part that changes to the part that does not change. The second pronunciation of **greasy** is \'grē-zē\ and the second pronunciation of **pajamas** is \pə-'jam-əz\.

If two or more entries are spelled the same and have the same pronunciation and end-of-line division, your dictionary will show the pronunciation of only the first of these entries.

> ¹**se·cure** \si-'kyùr\ *adj*...
> ²**secure** *vb*...

Many compound entries are made up of two or three separate words. If the dictionary does not show a pronunciation for all or part of such an entry, the missing pronunciation is the same as that for the individual word or words as given at their own entries.

> **milk shake** *n* : a drink made of milk, a flavoring syrup, and ice cream shaken or mixed thoroughly
> ¹**milk** \'milk\ *n*...
> ¹**shake** \'shāk\ *vb*...

As you can see, no pronunciation is shown for the entry **milk shake**. This means that the two words are pronounced just like the separate entries **milk** and **shake**.

Some dictionary entries have additional boldface words just after the entry word or at the end of the entry. (In upcoming lessons, we'll discuss the various reasons why this happens.) In such cases, the dictionary may show only part of the pronunciation. This means that the rest of the word is pronounced the same as part of the main entry.

TURN THE PAGE

15

post·pone \pōst-'pōn\ vb... —
  post·pone·ment \-mənt\ n
sub·head \'səb-ˌhed\ or sub·head·ing
  \-ˌhed-ing\ n

The pronunciation of **postponement** is
\pōst-'pōn-mənt\. **Subheading** is pronounced \'səb-ˌhed-ing\.

  Sometimes a boldface word at the end
of an entry will show no pronunciation at
all. In these cases the pronunciation of
the word is the same as the pronunciation of the main entry plus the pronunciation of a special word ending called a
suffix. The pronunciation of the suffix is
found at its own alphabetical place in the
dictionary.

rusty \'rəs-tē\ adj... — rust·i·ness n -
  ness \nəs\ n suffix...

In the example above, the entry **rustiness**
is pronounced \'rəs-tē-nəs\.

Be a Dictionary Detective

Use your dictionary to write the correct pronunciations for the following words
on the line provided. To do this exercise, you will have to look somewhere
other than the usual spot directly after the entry for all or part of the pronunciation.
You may have to look up two different words or parts and combine the
pronunciations. If you get stuck, reread the explanations above for clues.

nerve fiber

_____

²exhaust n

_____

extinguisher

_____

storminess

_____

conclusively

_____

managership

_____

eyeteeth

_____

outboard motor

_____

faithfully

_____

pled

_____

Variants

Some words have more than one correct spelling. In such cases, you may see a second or third spelling, also in **boldface** type, after the main entry word in the dictionary. These additional spellings are called **variant spellings** or simply **variants**.

> **scep·ter** *or* **scep·tre** \\'sep-tər\ *n* : a rod carried by a ruler as a sign of authority

This entry tells us that **scepter** and **scep-tre** are both accepted as correct spellings of the word.

Variant or Misspelling?

Each of the following pairs contains an entry word followed by a second spelling that may or may not be an accepted variant. Use your dictionary to find out if the second spelling is okay or not. Cross out the unacceptable spelling.

1.	**capital**	capitle	13.	**sulfur**	sulphur
2.	**barnacle**	barnickle	14.	**rhyme**	ryme
3.	**caliph**	calif	15.	**rigorous**	riggorous
4.	**caliper**	calipper	16.	**backward**	backwards
5.	**bogey**	bogie	17.	**syrup**	sirrup
6.	**ballast**	ballust	18.	**bluing**	blueing
7.	**garage**	garaje	19.	**fjord**	fiord
8.	**pom-pom**	pompon	20.	**incentive**	insentive
9.	**poinsettia**	poinsetta	21.	**fuse**	fuze
10	**peddler**	peddlar	22.	**mold**	mould
11.	**synapse**	sinapse	23.	**bark**	barque
12.	**salable**	saleable	24.	**barrel**	barel

All of the variants shown in the dictionary are correct, but some are used more often in writing than others. When you see two variants separated by *or*, you can assume that both forms are common. Usually they will simply be listed in alphabetical order, like **scepter** *or* **sceptre**.

If one form is slightly more common than the other, however, it will be listed first, even if that means the variants will be out of alphabetical order.

> **Gyp·sy** *or* **Gip·sy** \ˈjip-sē\ *n*…

In the previous example, the order of the variants tells you that **Gypsy** is used more often than **Gipsy**.

Sometimes you will also see a variant spelling shown after the word *also*.

> **pea** \ˈpē\ *n, pl* **peas** *also* **pease** \ˈpēz\…

The *also* tells you that the next spelling is much less common than the first, although it is still a correct spelling.

 ## Which Is Preferred?

Here are some words that have more than one spelling. The possibilities for each word are given in alphabetical order. One of the two choices given is preferred over the other. Circle the preferred spelling for each word—and pay careful attention! In several cases alternate forms exist for the plural or another form of the word. In these cases, the main entry is given in parentheses.

hoofs, hooves (hoof)

judgement, judgment

smelled, smelt (smell)

fungi, funguses (fungus)

shod, shoed (shoe)

ox, oxen (ox)

vacua, vacuums (vacuum)

quartet, quartette

juncoes, juncos (junco)

eerie, eery

encrust, incrust

shrank, shrunk (shrink)

hooray, hurrah

hooray, hurray

hurrah, hurray

distil, distill

among, amongst

biceps, bicepses (biceps)

Functional Labels

Frisky dogs happily romp and frolic.
(adjective)   (noun)   (adverb)   (verb)   (conjunction)   (verb)

Words are used in many different ways in a sentence. For example, if a word is used for the name of something (**car, house, rainbow**) it is called a **noun**. If it describes an action or a state of being (**run, stand, live, is**) the word is a **verb**. Words that show a quality of something (**tall, sleepy, fast**) are **adjectives**, and words that tell how, when, or where something happens (**quickly, very, yesterday, here**) are **adverbs**. **Pronouns (them, you, that)** are words which substitute for nouns, and **conjunctions (and, but, yet)** join two words or groups of words. **Prepositions (to, for, by)** combine with nouns and pronouns to form phrases that answer such questions as where?, how?, and which?, and **interjections (hi, adios, ouch)** stand alone and often show a feeling or a reaction to something rather than a meaning.

To show you how the various entry words are used, or how they function in a sentence, dictionaries use **functional labels** before the definitions. In Merriam-Webster dictionaries, these labels are usually abbreviations in slanting *italic* type, and they come right after the pronunciation—when one is shown—or immediately after the entry word.

> **sea·coast** \\'sē-ˌkōst\\ *n* : the shore of the sea
> **sitting room** *n* : LIVING ROOM

The eight most common functions, known as parts of **parts of speech**, are shown in the examples below.

noun	²**cereal** *n*...
verb	**sing** \\'sing\\ *vb*...
adjective	**hos·tile** \\'häst-l\\ *adj*...
adverb	²**just** *adv*...
pronoun	¹**none** \\'nən\\ *pron*...
conjunction	²**since** *conj*...
preposition	²**under** *prep*...
interjection	⁴**why** \\wī, hwī\\ *interj*...

Birds of a Feather

Each of the following words functions as one or more of the eight most common parts of speech. Write the words on the lines after the appropriate functional labels. Be careful—you'll have to write some words on more than one line, so check the dictionary carefully.

go	cloud	beside	these
anywhere	but	ouch	adorable
dictionary	by	strangely	because
because of	computer	well	she
between	hello	our	awful
or	remember	scorpion	oh
nor	you	succeed	into
brief	and	hey	run

vb _____

_____

n _____

_____

adj _____

_____

adv _____

_____

pron _____

_____

conj _____

_____

prep _____

_____

interj _____

_____

Homographs

Often you will find two, three, or more main entries that come one after another and are spelled exactly alike.

> **¹seal** \ˈsēl\ *n* **1 :** a sea mammal that swims with flippers, lives mostly in cold regions, mates and bears young on land, eats flesh, and is hunted for fur, hides, or oil **2 :** the soft dense fur of a northern seal
>
> **²seal** *n* **1 :** something (as a pledge) that makes safe or secure **2 :** a device with a cut or raised design or figure that can be stamped or pressed into wax or paper **3 :** a piece of wax stamped with a design and used to seal a letter or package **4 :** a stamp that may be used to close a letter or package <Christmas *seals*> **5 :** something that closes tightly **6 :** a closing that is tight and perfect
>
> **³seal** *vb* **1 :** to mark with a seal **2 :** to close or make fast with or as if with a seal — **seal·er** *n*

Although these words look alike, they are different words because they come from different sources and so have different meanings or because they are used in different ways in the sentence.

These similar entries are called **homographs** (from **homo-** "the same" and **-graph** "something written"—in this case "words written in the same way"). Each homograph has a small raised number before it. This number is used only in the dictionary entry to show that these are different words. The number is not used in writing the word.

Let's look closely at the homographs for **seal** to see just why they are different. The first entry, a noun, is defined as "a sea mammal." The second **seal** entry is also a noun, but this meaning, "something (as a pledge) that makes safe or secure," is completely different from the meaning of the first entry. The third homograph of **seal** is certainly related to the second, but **³seal** is a verb and, since it has a different use in the sentence, we show it as a different entry word.

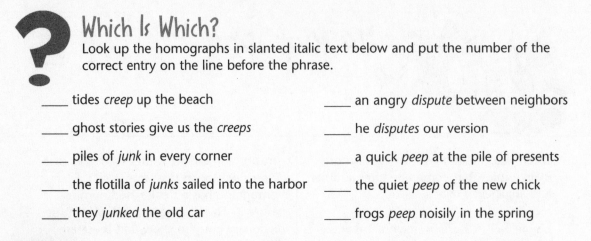

Which Is Which?

Look up the homographs in slanted italic text below and put the number of the correct entry on the line before the phrase.

____ tides *creep* up the beach

____ ghost stories give us the *creeps*

____ piles of *junk* in every corner

____ the flotilla of *junks* sailed into the harbor

____ they *junked* the old car

____ an angry *dispute* between neighbors

____ he *disputes* our version

____ a quick *peep* at the pile of presents

____ the quiet *peep* of the new chick

____ frogs *peep* noisily in the spring

Two for the Price of One

Here are 10 words that are entered as homographs in the dictionary. Choose the one word that makes sense in each sentence and fill in the blanks. Each word will appear in both of the blanks in only one sentence. (You may have to change the form of the word slightly to make a noun plural or to change the tense of a verb.)

base	can	express	fall	fan	light	low	right	tense

1. In the _____ the leaves _____ to the ground.

2. The basketball _____ _____ themselves in the hot auditorium.

3. The _____ answer is _____ in front of you.

4. The _____ of the statue is made of _____ metal.

5. She felt her muscles _____ as the situation grew _____.

6. _____ you open this _____ for me?

7. Let's turn off the _____ and _____ a candle.

8. He _____ a desire to have the package sent by _____ mail.

9. The cow's _____ is a _____ sound.

Inflected Forms

You have probably noticed by now that some dictionary entries contain other **boldface** words in addition to the first one (the main entry). Some of these boldface words are called inflected forms. In Merriam-Webster dictionaries, the inflected forms usually come after the function label in the entry.

> ¹**echo** \\'ek-ō\ *n, pl* **ech·oes**...
> ²**guide** *vb* **guid·ed; guid·ing**...
> **hot** \\'hät\ *adj* **hot·ter; hot·test**...

Inflected forms show the different forms that words can take depending on how they are being used. When we want to talk about more than one of something, English speakers use a special form of the noun called the **plural** form. **Echoes** is the plural form of **echo**. We also use special forms or **tenses** of verbs when we want to show that something has happened already (**guided**) or is happening now (**guiding**). And when we want to show how one thing is compared with another or with all others of the same kind, we use special forms of adjectives and adverbs called the **comparative** and **superlative** forms (**hotter** and **hottest**).

For most words, inflected forms are made in a regular way. Plurals are formed simply by adding *-s* or *-es* to the base word (one cat, two cat*s*; one box, two box*es*). Verb inflections are formed by adding *-ed* (yesterday I walk*ed* to school),

-ing (I was walk*ing* down the street), and *-s* or *-es* (she walk*s* her dog; he wash*es* his car). Comparative and superlative forms are formed by adding *-er* and *-est*, or with the words *more* and *most* (a fast*er* computer; the high*est* mountain; a *more* natural appearance; the *most* ridiculous story).

Dictionaries do not usually show regular inflections.

> **bri·gade** \bri-'gād\ *n* **1** : a body of soldiers consisting of two or more regiments...
> **dif·fer** \\'dif-ər\ *vb* **1** : to be not the same : be unlike...
> ¹**dull** \\'dəl\ *adj* **1** : mentally slow...

When you see entries like the examples **brigade**, **differ**, and **dull**, you will know that the inflected forms are regular. *Brigade* becomes *brigades; differ* becomes *differed, differing,* and *differs;* and *dull* becomes *duller* and *dullest.*

Dictionaries often do show the inflections, however, when they are formed in any way other than by simply adding a regular ending or when we think someone might have a question about how they are formed, spelled or pronounced.

> **deer** \\'dir\ *n, pl* **deer**...
> **go** \\'gō\ *vb* **went** \\'went\; **gone** \\'gȯn\; **go·ing** \\'gō-ing\; **goes**...
> **prop·er·ty** \\'präp-ərt-ē\ *n, pl* **prop·er·ties**...

Animals and Others

Here are 16 nouns that all form plurals in unusual ways. Some of them even have two plural forms. In the blank after each word write the plural form(s).

mantis	_____	knife	_____
fungus	_____	flamingo	_____
fez	_____	half	_____
dromedary	_____	quail	_____
trachea	_____	chassis	_____
reindeer	_____	goose	_____
fish	_____	hoof	_____
wolf	_____	octopus	_____

It Happened One Morning

Complete the paragraph below by filling in the blanks. Write the correct inflected forms of the verbs in parentheses.

Yesterday, I (wake) _____ up in the morning and (see) _____ a deer eating

outside my window. I also (hear) _____ a bird singing. It (sing) _____ until a

dog (come) _____ along and (scare) _____ it away. Then the dog (lie)

_____ down in the sun and (take) _____ a nap.

Good, Better, Best

Some of these adjectives form comparative and superlative forms in the regular way, and some do not. Write the correct comparative and superlative forms on the lines provided.

1. good	better best	7. zany	_____
2. bad	_____	8. windy	_____
3. green	_____	9. fat	_____
4. happy	_____	10. small	_____
5. wry	_____	11. narrow	_____
6. far	_____	12. muddy	_____

Usage Labels

In addition to functional labels, Merriam-Webster dictionaries use another kind of *italic* label to give information about how a word is used. **Usage labels** come after the functional labels or, if they apply only to a particular meaning, just before the beginning of the definition.

> **earth** \\'ərth\ *n* **1** : ²SOIL 1... **3** *often cap*
> : the planet that we live on
> **french fry** *n*, *often cap 1st F* : a strip of potato fried in deep fat...
> **ma** \\'mä, 'mȯ\ *n*, *often cap* : ¹MOTHER 1
> **no·el** \nō-'el\ *n* **1** : a Christmas carol
> **2** *cap* : the Christmas season

One of the things the usage label may tell you is whether or not a particular word is sometimes written with a capital letter. Whenever a word is always or usually written with a capital letter, it has a capital letter in the main entry.

> **Thurs·day** \\'thərz-dē\ *n* : the fifth day of the week

But some words are written with a small letter or a capital letter about equally often. These entries have an italic label *often cap*, like **ma** above. Other words are written with a capital letter in some meanings and not in others. These words are usually shown in the dictionary with a small first letter. The italic label tells you when the sense is always spelled with a

capital letter (*cap*, like sense **2** of **noel**) or very frequently spelled with a capital letter (*often cap*, like sense **3** of **earth**). Can you tell what the usage label at the entry **french fry** means? If you would expect to see the word sometimes spelled *French fry* you're absolutely right.

Another thing the usage labels can tell you is whether a word or particular meaning is limited in use. One kind of word with limited use is a word that is not used much anymore although it was quite common a long time ago.

> **thou** \\'thau̇\ *pron*, *singular*, *archaic*
> : YOU...

Thou is entered in the dictionary because you may sometimes see it in very old writings—in some versions of the Bible, for example.

The last kind of usage label tells you that a certain word or meaning is most commonly used in a limited area of the English-speaking world.

> **²lift** *n* **1** : the amount that may be lifted at one time : LOAD... **4** *chiefly British*
> : ELEVATOR 2...

Here you see that meaning **4** is labeled *chiefly British*. This means that the word in this meaning is used more often in Great Britain than in the United States.

Getting It Right

Pick the correct choice to complete the sentence and
write the letter in the blank.

1. The word *dalmatian* is _____.

 a) always capitalized   b) never capitalized   c) often capitalized

2. When the word *treasury* is capitalized, it refers to _____.

 a) a pirate's chest   b) a government department

 c) a place where money collected is kept and paid out

3. The adjective *bonny* is _____.

 a) often capitalized   b) archaic   c) used more often in Britain

4. The two most usual stylings of the verb *x-ray* are _____.

 a) x-ray and X-ray   b) x-Ray and X-Ray   c) X-Ray and X-ray

5. The pronoun *ye* is _____.

 a) often capitalized   b) archaic   c) used more often in Britain

6. The noun *thoroughbred* is capitalized when it means _____.

 a) a fine person   b) a purebred animal   c) a breed of racing horses

7. The word *mercury* is _____.

 a) always capitalized   b) capitalized in a specific use   c) never capitalized

8. The word *norman* is _____.

 a) sometimes capitalized   b) almost always capitalized   c) archaic

9. The word *soloist* is _____.

 a) British   b) usually capitalized   c) not usually capitalized

10. The label at *plaster of paris* is _____.

 a) often cap 2d P   b) archaic   c) often cap 1st P

11. The letters of the alphabet (*a, b, c,* etc.) are _____.

 a) often capitalized   b) capitalized in a specific use   c) never capitalized

12. The word *north* is sometimes capitalized when it is a(n) _____.

 a) adjective   b) adverb   c) noun

Definitions—Meaning

Definitions are what many people consider the most important part of the dictionary, because meanings are what people usually think of when they think of a dictionary.

Every definition in Merriam-Webster dictionaries starts with a **boldface** colon (:). The colon is used for each definition, even when there are two or more definitions for the same meaning.

> **in·trep·id** \in-ˈtrep-əd\ *adj* : feeling no fear : BOLD — **in·trep·id·ly** *adv*

The entry **intrepid**, for example, has two colons and two definitions. The definitions ("feeling no fear" and "bold") have the same basic meaning, but each is using different words to explain the same thing. (We'll explain why "bold" is in all capital letters in lesson 15.)

Many of the words entered in the dictionary have more than one meaning or **sense**, however. These separate meanings are shown by boldface numbers placed in front of the colons.

> **mill·er** \ˈmil-ər\ *n* **1** : a person who works in or runs a flour mill **2** : a moth whose wings seem to be covered with flour or dust

There may be times when you will look up a word and be unsure which of several senses is the right one for the use you are checking. In such cases, you'll need to look closely at the definitions to see which is the best fit for the situation.

Suppose you are reading the sentence "A miller flies by and lands on a lampshade" and you are not certain what *miller* means. You look up the word in your dictionary and find two different meaning. How can you tell which is the right one? Take a look at the sentence again. Would it make sense for "a person who works in or runs a flour mill" to fly by and land on a lampshade? Probably not. But that certainly sounds like something "a moth whose wings seem to be covered with flour or dust" might do.

Look It Up

Look up each word and write the letter of the correct meaning in the blank.

1. baste _____
   a) a starting place or goal in various games   b) to moisten while roasting
   c) to lie or relax in pleasantly warm surroundings   d) to hit very hard

2. dell _____
   a) to dig deeply into the earth   b) a small valley   c) an indefinite amount
   d) lacking brightness or luster

3. frazzle _____
   a) a tired or nervous condition   b) filled with fear   c) not controlled by others
   d) recently hatched or very young fishes

4. mart _____
   a) to set apart by a line or boundary   b) gloom, darkness
   c) the state of being merry or happy as shown by laughter   d) a trading place

Context Is Key

Which definition best fits the italic word in the phrases below?
Write the letter in the blank.

1. reading the ancient *classics* _____
   a) a written work or author of ancient Greece or Rome
   b) a great work of art   c) something outstanding of its kind

2. *scored* the wood with a knife _____
   a) to set down in an account   b) to keep the score in a game
   c) to cut or mark with a line, scratch, or notch

3. legally *bound* to report the incident _____
   a) tied or fastened with or as if with bands   b) required by law or duty
   c) covered with binding

Definitions— Historical Order

How do dictionary editors decide which meaning to list first? In Merriam-Webster dictionaries, the order is **historical**, which means it reflects the order in which the different meanings came into use.

> **skim** \\'skim\\ *vb* **skimmed; skim·ming**
> **1** : to clean a liquid of scum or float-ing substance : remove (as cream or film) from the top part of a liquid
> **2** : to read or examine quickly and not thoroughly **3** : to throw so as to skip along the surface of water **4** : to pass swiftly or lightly over

Let's look at meaning number **1** of **skim**. This meaning first came into use in English many centuries ago, and through the years it gained a more specific use, that of taking the cream off milk. This specific use is shown as the second defini-tion at meaning **1**. The second definition does not change the original meaning; it only adds a little.

Meaning **2** of **skim** seems to have come into use as a figure of speech. If you think of a spoon barely touching the surface of water or milk or going just under the surface to scoop off something,

you realize that the scoop is only taking off what can be seen on the surface. Most of the liquid remains behind. By first applying the word *skim* to reading or examining something and only getting what could be seen "on the surface" without going more deeply into the work, someone was using *skim* as a figure of speech. As more and more people used the word in this way, it came to have a set meaning.

Meaning **3**, which developed after meanings **1** and **2**, seems to have come from the first meaning in a similar way. This time, though, the idea of "just touching" a surface was the one that carried over to the act of causing rocks or other objects to bounce along the surface of a body of water.

Can you guess at how meaning **4** came into use? Here it seems the meaning moved one more step away, from the idea of "just touching the surface" to that of "just missing the surface."

With the entry **skim**, you can see just how the word grew from one meaning to four. And the arrangement of the four meanings in historical order lets you follow that growth.

Tried and True

Which meaning is the oldest? Write the answer in the blank.

1. bowl _____
   a) to hit with or as if with something rolled   b) to move rapidly and smoothly
   as rolling   c) to roll a ball in bowling

2. crust _____
   a) the hardened outside surface of bread   b) the pastry cover of a pie
   c) the outer part of the earth's surface

3. gentility _____
   a) the qualities of a well-bred person   b) good manners
   c) good birth and family

4. reserve _____
   a) caution in one's words and behavior   b) something stored or available
   for future use   c) an area of land set apart

Cutting Edge

Which meaning is the most recent? Write the answer in the blank.

1. apt _____
   a) quick to learn   b) having a tendency   c) just right

2. kink _____
   a) cramp   b) a short tight twist or curl
   c) an imperfection that makes something hard to use or work

3. plain _____
   a) clear to the mind   b) not handsome or beautiful
   c) having no pattern or decoration

4. raw _____
   a) not trained or experienced   b) not cooked   c) unpleasantly damp or cold

Synonyms and Cross-references

In Merriam-Webster dictionaries, you will often see words in definitions that are printed entirely in SMALL CAPITAL letters. Any word in small capital letters following a boldface colon is a **synonym** of the entry word. This is to say, it has the same or nearly the same meaning as the entry word.

> **per·haps** \pər-'haps\ *adv* : possibly but not certainly : MAYBE

We see the synonym MAYBE in the entry **perhaps**, for example. *Maybe* is a word that also means "possibly but not certainly," just as *perhaps* does.

Sometimes an entry is defined only by a synonym.

> **mail carrier** *n* : LETTER CARRIER

In the entry **mail carrier**, LETTER CARRIER is a **cross-reference** referring you to the entry **letter carrier**. There you will find a definition that also applies to **mail carrier**.

> **letter carrier** *n* : a person who delivers mail

You now know that the word *mail carrier* means "a person who delivers mail." Cross-references save space in dictionaries because they take up less room than printing the full definition in two places.

Sometimes you will see a number used as part of the cross-reference, as at the entry **feign**.

> **feign** \'fān\ *vb* : PRETEND 2

The cross-reference to PRETEND 2 tells you that the definition found at sense 2 of **pretend** also fits **feign**.

> **pre·tend** \pri-'tend\ *vb* **1** : to make believe : SHAM **2** : to put forward as true something that is not true <*pretend* friendship> — **pre·tend·er** *n*

The entry word and the synonym will always have the same part of speech. Thus, if the synonym of a verb is an entry with two or more homographs, you will always know that the right entry will be the homograph that is a verb. Nevertheless, your dictionary helps you by showing the proper homograph number at the cross-reference when necessary.

> **prick·er** \'prik-ər\ *n* : [1]PRICKLE 1

In the entry **pricker**, the cross-reference is telling you to look at meaning **1** of the first homograph of **prickle**.

> [1]**prick·le** \'prik-əl\ *n* **1** : a small sharp point (as a thorn) **2** : a slight stinging pain

Synonyms, Synonyms

Use your dictionary to find the synonyms for the words given here.
Write the synonyms on the lines next to the words.

engender _____

hallway _____

bring about_____

predicament _____

thickset _____

insignificant _____

habitual _____

malt _____

inwardly _____

shimmer _____

inkling _____

mote _____

One Step, Two Step

Use your dictionary and your cross-reference skills to identify the correct
definition for the following words. Write the letter in the blank.

1. beau _____
   a) a regular male companion of a girl or woman   b) a beautiful girl or woman
   c) a candy with a soft coating and a creamy center

2. cinder _____
   a) a North American tree that has needles and small egg-shaped cones
   b) a red mineral consisting of a sulfide of mercury
   c) the waste left after the melting of ores and the separation of metal from them

3. hoarfrost _____
   a) to cover with frost or with something suggesting frost
   b) temperature cold enough to cause freezing   c) a covering of tiny ice crystals

4. incline _____
   a) upward or downward slant   b) a piece of slanting ground
   c) a turn for the worse

5. norm _____
   a) to amount to usually   b) something usual in a group, class, or series
   c) being ordinary or usual

Verbal Illustrations

At times you may look up a word in your dictionary and understand the definition but still be unsure about the right way to use the word. Sometimes the several meanings are similar, but the ways in which the word is actually used in a sentence are quite different.

To help you understand the more difficult words and usages, Merriam-Webster dictionaries include brief phrases or sentences called **verbal illustrations** at many definitions. A verbal illustration shows you a typical use of the word. It comes after the definition and is enclosed in pointed brackets, like this < >. The entry word, or an inflection of it, appears in the verbal illustration in italic type.

At the entry **snap**, for example, most of the definitions have verbal illustrations to show how the word is used in each meaning.

¹**snap** \'snap\ *vb* **snapped; snap·ping**
1 : to grasp or grasp at something suddenly with the mouth or teeth <fish *snapping* at the bait> **2 :** to grasp at something eagerly <*snapped* at the chance to go> **3 :** to get, take, or buy at once <*snap* up a bargain> **4 :** to speak or utter sharply or irritably <*snap* out a command> **5 :** to break or break apart suddenly and often with a cracking noise <the branch *snapped*> **6 :** to make or cause to make a sharp or crackling sound <*snap* a whip> **7 :** to close or fit in place with a quick movement <the lid *snapped* shut> **8 :** to put into or remove from a position suddenly or with a snapping sound <*snap* off a switch> **9 :** to close by means of snaps or fasteners **10 :** to act or be acted on with snap <*snapped* to attention> **11 :** to take a snapshot of

Which Phrase Fits?

Pick the verbal illustration that is the best match for the meaning shown. Write the letter in the blank.

1. dishonest _____
    a) <a *crooked* path>   b) <the picture is *crooked*>   c) <a *crooked* card game>

2. learn _____
    a) <good readers *pick up* new words from their reading>
    b) <*pick up* a bargain>   c) <*picked up* the outlaw's trail>

TURN THE PAGE

3. to cause to ignite by scratching _____
   a) <the ship *struck* a rock>   b) <*strike* a match>   c) <*strike* a bargain>

4. to provide temporary quarters for _____
   a) <*lodge* a guest for the night>   b) <we *lodged* in motels>   c) <*lodge* a complaint>

5. not holding public office_____
   a) <*private* property>   b) <a *private* citizen>   c) <a *private* meeting>

6. good working condition _____
   a) <a list of names in alphabetical *order*>   b) <the telephone is out of *order*>
   c) <place an *order* for groceries>

Which Meaning Matches?

Pick the meaning that is the best match for the verbal illustration shown.
Write the letter in the blank.

1. <don't *scramble* up those papers> _____
   a) to work hard to win or escape something   b) to mix together in disorder
   c) to cook eggs by stirring them while frying

2. <an *original* mind> _____
   a) of or relating to the origin or beginning   b) not copied from anything else
   c) able to think up new things

3. <*plead* illness> _____
   a) to argue for or against   b) to offer as an excuse or an apology
   c) to make an earnest appeal

4. <we *split* the profit> _____
   a) to divide lengthwise   b) to burst or break apart
   c) to divide into shares or sections

5. <*hot* jewels> _____
   a) recently stolen   b) radioactive   c) easily excited

6. <*burned* my finger> _____
   a) to destroy by fire or heat   b) to make or produce by fire or heat
   c) to injure by fire or heat

Usage Notes

The *italic* usage labels that come before definitions and the verbal illustrations after the definitions are two ways that Merriam-Webster dictionaries give you extra information about how words are used. And there's a third way—**usage notes** following definitions. Usage notes are short phrases that are separated from the definition by a dash. They tell you how or when the entry word is used.

> **blast off** \blas-ˈtȯf\ *vb* : to take off — used of vehicles using rockets for power
>
> **cas·ta·net** \ˌkas-tə-ˈnet\ *n* : a rhythm instrument that consists of two small ivory, wooden, or plastic shells fastened to the thumb and clicked by the fingers in time to dancing and music — usually used in pl.
>
> ²**cheer** *vb*... **4** : to grow or be cheerful — usually used with *up*

The usage note at **blast off** tells you that the word is usually used in a particular situation. The note at **castanet** tells you that the word is most often used in the plural form and with a plural verb, although it is defined as a singular. (If the word was *always* plural, it would have been entered as **castanets** and defined as plural.) Usage notes like the one at **cheer** tell you what words are usually used with the entry word in a sentence. In this case, the expression is usually *cheer up*.

Sometimes dictionaries use usage notes in place of definitions. This is done when the way the word is used is more important than what the word means.

> ²**both** *conj* — used before two words or phrases connected with *and* to stress that each is included <*both* New York and London>

We also use a usage note in place of a definition for all interjections, which usually express a feeling or reaction to something rather than a meaning.

> **amen** \ˈā-ˈmen, ˈä-\ *interj* — used to express agreement (as after a prayer or a statement of opinion)

Usual Uses

For each definition, pick the form of the word that is most usual.
Write the letter in the blank.

1. open seats for people to watch from _____
   a) bleacher   b) bleachers   c) Bleacher   d) Bleachers

2. an instrument with two adjustable legs _____
   a) Caliper   b) Calipers   c) caliper   d) calipers

3. to grow or be cheerful _____
   a) cheer around   b) cheer down   c) cheer up   d) cheer out

4. being a result _____
   a) due of   b) due from   c) due   d) due to

Using Usage

Choose the phrase that best completes the sentence.
Write the letter in the blank.

1. The preposition *in* can be _____.
   a) used to show a state or condition   b) used to indicate a particular place or time
   c) used to show who or what is to receive something

2. The word *would* is often _____.
   a) capitalized   b) used with *up*   c) used to show politeness

3. The interjection *adios* is _____.
   a) used instead of hello   b) used instead of goodbye   c) used in France

4. The interjection *alas* is _____.
   a) used by pirates   b) used to express excitement and surprise
   c) used to express unhappiness, pity, or worry

Undefined Entries

Some entries in the dictionary have **boldface** words at the end, like at the entry **sour**.

> ¹**sour** \ˈsau̇r\ *adj* **1** : having an acid taste **2** : having become acid through spoiling <*sour* milk> **3** : suggesting decay <a *sour* smell> **4** : not pleasant or friendly <a *sour* look> **5** : acid in reaction <*sour* soil> — **sour·ish** \-ish\ *adj* — **sour·ly** *adv* — **sour·ness** *n*

These boldface words are **undefined run-on entries**. Each is shown without a definition of its own, but you can easily discover the meaning by simply combining the meaning of the base word (the main entry) and the added-on part (the suffix). For example, **sourish** is simply **sour** plus **-ish** ("somewhat") and so means "somewhat sour"; **sourly** is simply **sour** plus **-ly** ("in a specified manner") and so means "in a sour manner"; and **sourness** is **sour** plus **-ness** ("state : condition") and so means "the state or condition of being sour."

Your dictionary includes as run-on entries only words whose meanings you should have no trouble figuring out. If a word comes from a main entry plus a suffix but has a meaning that is not easy to understand from the meanings of the two parts, the dictionary will enter and define it at its own alphabetical place.

Words Plus

Each of the words below is entered as a run-on entry of a main entry word in your dictionary. Match the words to the definitions in the right column. Write the number of the correct definition in the blank before the word.

___ baldness

___ bravely

___ copiously

___ fruitlessly

___ genuineness

___ guileful

___ hairless

___ intelligibly

___ invisibly

___ judiciously

___ juggler

___ lavishly

___ lopsidedness

___ motherhood

___ nonsensically

___ observantly

___ prowler

___ quibbler

___ ruthlessness

___ scatterbrained

___ stalked

___ timidly

___ uncivilly

___ valueless

1. without a threadlike growth from the skin of a person or lower animal

2. the state or condition of being cruel

3. in a manner that is impossible to see

4. the state or condition of lacking a natural covering

5. one who finds fault especially over unimportant points

6. having a slender supporting structure

7. one who moves about quietly and secretly like a wild animal hunting prey

8. in a manner characterized by good judgment

9. in an abundant manner

10. in a manner possible to understand

11. not having worth, usefulness, or importance in comparison with something else

12. in a manner that makes no sense

13. in an unsuccessful manner

14. characterized by sly trickery

15. in an impolite manner

16. in a manner suggesting a lack of fear

17. in a watchful manner

18. in an extravagant manner

19. having the characteristics of a flighty, thoughtless person

20. the state or condition of being just what it seems to be

21. the state or condition of being a female parent

22. in a manner suggesting a lack of courage or self-confidence

23. one who keeps several things moving in the air at the same time

24. the state or condition of being unbalanced

Synonym Paragraphs

In lesson 15 we discussed how synonyms (words that have the same or nearly the same meaning) appear in some definitions in SMALL CAPITAL letters. Merriam-Webster dictionaries handle synonyms in another way too. At the end of some entries, you will see a special kind of cross-reference like the one at **superb**.

su·perb \su̇-'pərb\ *adj* : outstandingly excellent, impressive, or beautiful **synonyms** see SPLENDID

The direction **"synonyms** see SPLENDID" means "for a discussion of synonyms that includes **superb**, see the entry **splendid**." Such discussions of synonyms are called **synonym paragraphs**.

splen·did \'splen-dəd\ *adj* **1** : having or showing splendor : BRILLIANT **2** : impressive in beauty, excellence, or magnificence <did a *splendid* job> <a *splendid* palace> **3** : GRAND **4** — **splen·did·ly** *adv*

synonyms SPLENDID, GLORIOUS, and SUPERB mean very impressive. SPLENDID suggests that something is far above the ordinary in excellence or magnificence <what a *splendid* idea> <a *splendid* jewel>. GLORIOUS suggests that something is radiant with light or beauty <a *glorious* sunset>. SUPERB suggests the highest possible point of magnificence or excellence <a *superb* museum> <the food was *superb*>

Synonyms can often be substituted freely for one another in a sentence because they mean basically the same thing. Sometimes synonyms have meanings that are almost the same, but not exactly. They cannot always be substituted for one another. Synonyms may differ slightly in what they suggest to the reader—in the image they call to mind. These suggested meanings may make one synonym a better choice than another in certain situations.

Synonym paragraphs explain the little differences between synonyms. Any of the three words in the paragraph following the entry **splendid** would be satisfactory in the examples given to indicate something impressive. But over the years people have come to think of the word *glorious* as more suited to describing something where light or beauty is involved, while *splendid* and *superb* are used of other things. And something described as superb is often thought of as more wonderful than something merely splendid.

Shades of Meaning

Find the synonym paragraph in your dictionary for each set of words listed below. Read the paragraph carefully, then choose the word that is the best fit for each sentence.

> enjoyment, joy, pleasure / mend, patch, repair
> calm, peaceful, tranquil / task, duty, job

1. Her face was shining with _____ after learning that she had won

   the contest.

   He takes personal _____ in doing a good job.

   The bad weather did not take away from our _____ of the picnic.

2. The old clock took many hours to _____.

   I thought my favorite jeans were ruined forever, but Mom showed me how to

   _____ the hole with a scrap of material.

   I'll have to _____ that dress if I want to wear it to the wedding.

3. The _____ beauty of a mountain view always puts me in a relaxed mood.

   It is important to remain _____ in an emergency.

   We enjoyed a _____ dinner after the fussy children went to bed.

4. We will have to work hard if we want to get the _____ done in time.

   The teacher assigned me the _____ of collecting everyone's assignments.

   If you have a pet, it is your _____ to be responsible and take good

   care of it.

Phrases

The last kind of **boldface** entry you will find in your Merriam-Webster dictionary is the **defined run-on phrase**. These phrases are groups of words that, when used together, have a special meaning that is more than just the sum of the ordinary meanings of each word.

> ¹**stand** \'stand\ *vb* **stood** \'stŭd\; **stand·ing 1 :** to be in or take a vertical position on one's feet **2 :** to take up or stay in a specified position or condition <*stands* first in the class> <*stands* accused> <machines *standing* idle> **3 :** to have an opinion <how do you *stand* on taxes?> **4 :** to rest, remain, or set in a usually vertical position <*stand* the box in the corner> **5 :** to be in a specified place <the house *stands* on the hill> **6 :** to stay in effect <the order still *stands*> **7 :** to put up with : ENDURE <can't *stand* pain> **8 :** UNDERGO <*stand* trial> **9 :** to perform the duty of <*stand* guard> — **stand by :** to be or remain loyal or true to <*stand by* a promise> — **stand for 1 :** to be a symbol for : REPRESENT **2 :** to put up with : PERMIT <won't *stand for* any nonsense>

The defined run-on phrases are placed at the end of the entry that is the first major word of the phrase. Normally this will be the first noun or verb rather than an adjective or preposition. The phrases run on at **stand** all begin with the entry word **stand**. But some run-on phrases will not have the major word at the beginning of the phrase. Keep in mind that the phrase will be entered at the first major word in the phrase. This word is usually a noun or a verb. Where do you think you would find the phrases **do away with, in the doghouse,** and **on fire**? If you said at the verb **do,** at the noun **doghouse,** and at the noun **fire,** then you understand how the phrases are entered and where you should look for them.

Where to find the phrase **read between the lines** may puzzle you at first, since it contains both a verb (read) and a noun (lines). But if you remember that the phrase will be entered at the *first* major word, in this case the verb **read,** you should have no trouble finding the phrases entered in this dictionary.

turn turtle

Eureka!

Here are some run-on phrases from your dictionary. In the blank next to each phrase write the main entry word where you found the phrase.

_____ 1. put forward

_____ 2. out of the blue

_____ 3. take part

_____ 4. in spite of

_____ 5. from time to time

_____ 6. get one's goat

_____ 7. make believe

_____ 8. in common

_____ 9. beside oneself

_____ 10. on the contrary

_____ 11. turn the trick

_____ 12. out of hand

_____ 13. play hooky

_____ 14. follow suit

_____ 15. on the spot

_____ 16. by no means

What Does It Mean?

Pick the choice that gives the correct meaning for the following run-on phrases. Write the letter in the blank.

1. get ahead _____
   a) to buy property   b) to push and shove   c) to achieve success

2. better part _____
   a) more than half   b) superior component   c) favorite food

3. at every turn _____
   a) all the time   b) where to stop   c) the corners of a square figure

4. get wind of _____
   a) feel a draught   b) fly a kite   c) become aware of

5. set about _____
   a) place wickets on a croquet course   b) begin to do   c) run away

6. on tap _____
   a) liquid   b) inexpensive   c) available

7. read between the lines _____
   a) read carefully   b) hallucinate   c) understand more than is directly stated

Word History Paragraphs

One of the important jobs of people who study words and write dictionaries is finding out where the words we use every day in English came from. Some of our words are made up by people using the language today. Whenever a scientist discovers a new element or creates a new drug, for example, he or she makes up a name for it.

But most of the words in the English language have a long history. They usually can be traced back to other words in languages older than English. Many of these languages, like ancient Greek and Latin, are no longer spoken today. The study of the origins of words can be fascinating, for many of our words have very interesting stories behind them.

Some Merriam-Webster dictionaries

(especially those that have been published for young students) include special short **word history paragraphs** like the one at **surly**. These paragraphs discuss the interesting stories of word origins and trace the development of meanings over the years.

> **sur·ly** \'sər-lē\ *adj* **sur·li·er; sur·li·est**
>   : having a mean rude disposition
>   : UNFRIENDLY
>
> **Word History** The word *surly* comes from the word *sir*. Long ago, some Englishmen who had the title *Sir* became too proud of it. Such men were called *sirly*, a word that meant "overbearing" and "arrogant." Over the years the spelling changed to *surly* and came to be used of anyone who is rude and unfriendly.

Where in the World?

For each of the words that follow, write the language that was its *earliest* source.

1. _____ academy
2. _____ admiral
3. _____ zest
4. _____ bugle
5. _____ lord
6. _____ flamingo
7. _____ chameleon
8. _____ amethyst
9. _____ robot
10. _____ molar

11. _____ nickel
12. _____ gorgeous
13. _____ hazard
14. _____ lunatic
15. _____ dachshund
16. _____ uproar
17. _____ ballot
18. _____ December
19. _____ lady
20. _____ panic

Looking Back

Write the number of the correct description on the right next to each word on the left.

_____ ukulele	1. from a Latin word meaning "white"
_____ magazine	2. from an old word meaning "doctor"
_____ éclair	3. from the name of a saint
_____ canary	4. from a Hawaiian word meaning "jumping flea"
_____ chameleon	5. named for what Romans called the "dog islands"
_____ dog days	6. from the sound it makes
_____ buffalo	7. from a Dutch word meaning "donkey"
_____ hippopotamus	8. from a Greek word meaning "little crane"
_____ dismal	9. from the name of a city in France
_____ denim	10. from a Spanish word meaning "a stray animal"
_____ mustang	11. in French, "flash of lightning"
_____ easel	12. from a Latin word meaning "flame"
_____ escape	13. named for the rising of a star
_____ filbert	14. from Latin, Spanish, and Italian for "wild ox"
_____ flamingo	15. from the Greek for "river horse"
_____ leech	16. from Arabic and French sources that meant "storehouse"
_____ lunatic	17. from Greek words meaning "on the ground" and "lion"
_____ geranium	18. from a French word meaning "to go over again with a harrow"
_____ nice	19. based on the idea of someone slipping out of a cloak
_____ katydid	20. from the Latin word for "moon"
_____ candidate	21. once meant "stupid" or "foolish"
_____ rehearse	22. from the Latin for "evil days"

How to Use a Thesaurus

What Is a Thesaurus?

A **thesaurus** is basically a collection of word lists. The words are grouped together with other words that are either the same or opposite in meaning. A person usually uses a thesaurus when he or she has one word in mind and is looking for a word that is like it or in direct contrast to it.

Some of the words grouped together in a thesaurus are very similar to one another. Others are alike in some ways and not in others. For example, at the thesaurus entry **car** you will find the words *auto* and *automobile*. Both of these are very close to *car* in meaning. But you will also find words like *sedan* and *station wagon*. These words are used for specific types of cars. You might also find a word like *wreck*, which can refer to a car in a particular condition (the condition of having been badly damaged in a crash). The same basic idea applies to opposite words. You will find some words that are exactly opposite and some that are almost opposite.

Some of the things you've learned about Merriam-Webster dictionaries also apply to Merriam-Webster thesauruses. The entries of the thesaurus are arranged in alphabetical order. Each entry is introduced by a **boldface** word that sticks out a bit into the margin. You will see *italic* functional labels indicating how each entry word is used in a sentence, verbal illustrations in pointy brackets < >, and cross-reference words in SMALL CAPITAL letters directing you to other entries. Homographs (words that are spelled the same but come from different sources or have different part-of-speech labels) have separate entries. And entries for words having more than one meaning are divided into meaning groups (or senses) introduced by boldface numbers.

But thesaurus entries look quite different from dictionary entries in other ways. Here are some sample thesaurus entries.

often *adv* many times <we called *often* but still could not reach you>
  syn again and again, frequently, much, oft, oftentimes, ofttimes, over and over, repeatedly, time and again
  idiom a number of times, many a time, many times over, time and time again
  con infrequently, rarely; now and then, occasionally
  ant seldom
oftentimes *adv syn* see OFTEN
ofttimes *adv syn* see OFTEN

The entry **often** is a **main entry**. Each main entry in the thesaurus is made up of a boldface headword followed by a functional label, a meaning number if needed, a meaning core with a short verbal illustration, and a list of synonyms. Most of the time the main entry also

TURN THE PAGE

includes other kinds of lists as at **often**. (We'll explain about each kind of list in upcoming lessons.) **Oftentimes** and **ofttimes** are **secondary entries**. Each secondary entry in the thesaurus includes a cross-reference that directs you to a main entry where you will find more information.

Find the Misfit

Each set of words below includes one word that would NOT likely show up in a thesaurus entry with the other words. Circle the word that doesn't fit the group. Remember that the words do not have to be exactly the same, but they should have something in common—or they may be opposites. Use your dictionary if you are uncertain about the meaning of any of the words.

1. tiny teeny tawny huge miniature

2. run sprint scamper scrawl scurry

3. criticize blame censor condemn saturate

4. engrave carve idolize etch inscribe

5. humble vainglorious conceited indelible meek

6. commotion illumination agitation turmoil calm

7. disconsolate downcast happy despondent dexterous

8. rusty rural urban rustic pastoral

9. important unimportant significant premature momentous

10. everlasting eternal effectual endless perpetual

Dictionary Versus Thesaurus

Will you find the following dictionary features in your thesaurus as well? Circle *yes* or *no*.

1. verbal illustrations   yes   no   6. usage paragraphs   yes   no

2. pronunciation symbols   yes   no   7. cross-reference words   yes   no

3. sense numbers   yes   no   8. alphabetical order   yes   no

4. word history paragraphs yes   no   9. functional labels   yes   no

5. homographs   yes   no   10. meanings   yes   no

Meaning Cores and Verbal Illustrations

In lesson 22 we said that a thesaurus is basically a collection of word lists, and this is true. But the primary entries in Merriam-Webster thesauruses also include short definitions, or **meaning cores**. The meaning core indicates the sense or area of meaning in which a group of words is synonymous.

> **calm** *adj* **1** free from storm or rough activity <the wind died and the sea became *calm*>
> **syn** halcyon, hushed, placid, quiet, still, stilly, untroubled
> **rel** inactive, quiescent, reposing, resting; pacific, smooth, tranquil, unruffled
> **idiom** calm as a millpond, still as death
> **con** agitated, disturbed, perturbed, restless, turbulent, uneasy
> **ant** stormy

The meaning core for **calm 1**, for example, is "free from storm or rough activity." This is the meaning of *calm* for which the words *halcyon, hushed, placid, quiet, still, stilly,* and *untroubled* are synonyms.

   In some cases, a meaning core is followed by a typical object in parentheses.

> **express** *vb*... **2** to give expression to (as a thought, an opinion, or an emotion)

The material in parentheses in the entry **express** tells you that the word is usually used in connection with "a thought, an opinion, or an emotion" when it is used in this sense.

   A meaning core may also have a usage note introduced by a dash.

> **yet** *adv* **1** beyond this — used as an intensive to stress the comparative degree

Some interjections express feelings but cannot be given a simple meaning. In such cases, the meaning core itself may be replaced by a usage note (as in the dictionary).

> **good–bye** *interj* — used as a conventional expression of good wishes at parting

Each meaning core is followed by a verbal illustration enclosed in pointed brackets.

> <the wind died and the sea became *calm*>

This verbal illustration shows a typical use of the headword **calm** in the sense defined by meaning core 1.

Matchmaker

Match each meaning core on the left with a word on the right.
Write the number of the correct word in the blank.

_____ something uttered or proposed that seems senseless or absurd

_____ a table, frame, or case with a sloping or horizontal surface especially for writing

_____ to give one thing in exchange for another with an expectation of gain

_____ to find fault incessantly

_____ heard or perceived with the ear

_____ to cause to cease burning

_____ one engaged in sailing or handling a ship

1. nag

2. extinguish

3. desk

4. aural

5. nonsense

6. mariner

7. trade

Matchmaker

Match each meaning core on the left with a verbal illustration on the right.
Write the number of the correct verbal illustration in the blank.

_____ to strike or to fill with fear or dread

_____ dry or rough in sound

_____ marked by a heavy oppressive quality of air

_____ a state or time of beauty, freshness, and vigor

_____ to drive or force someone out

_____ lacking vim and energy

_____ marked by kindly courtesy

1. <the *bloom* of youth>

2. <the puppy was *frightened* by the unfamiliar noises>

3. <*eject* an intruder from one's house>

4. <her *gracious* attitude toward those around her>

5. <doing the job in a slow and *languid* manner>

6. <developed a *hoarse* cough>

7. <a *stuffy* room that needed airing>

Synonyms and Related Words

The next part of the main entry of your thesaurus is the list of synonyms.

> **safety** *n* the quality, state, or condition of being safe <there's *safety* in numbers>
> **syn** assurance, safeness, security

In Merriam-Webster thesauruses, synonyms are words that share a basic meaning with the entry word. The synonyms may have other meanings as well, but they must have at least one meaning in common with the entry word and the other synonyms in the list. The meaning core that comes before the synonym list tells you what meaning is shared by the words in the list.

In many entries, the synonym list is followed by a list of **related words**.

> **easily** *adj* **1** without discomfort, difficulty, or reluctance <*easily* translated the document>
> **syn** effortlessly, facilely, freely, lightly, readily, smoothly, well
> **rel** competently, dexterously, efficiently, fluently, handily, simply

Related words are words that are almost but not quite synonyms.

If you are looking for a word that is very close in meaning to a given word, the synonym list is the place to look. But if you are looking for a word that is only somewhat similar, you should look at the list of related words.

Bet on a Set

Select the set of synonyms that is the best match for each meaning core below. Write the appropriate letter in the blank.

1. something less than the whole to which it belongs _____
   a) piece, portion, section   b) total, whole, sum   c) small, little, petite

2. lacking a definite plan, purpose, or pattern _____
   a) foolish, silly, witless   b) comic, funny, laughable   c) aimless, haphazard, random

3. demanding great toil and effort _____
   a) apt, likely, prone   b) arduous, hard, difficult   c) petty, paltry, trivial

TURN THE PAGE

4. being smaller than what is normal, necessary, or desirable _____
   a) plaintive, mournful, melancholy   b) eloquent, expressive, significant
   c) scanty, skimpy, meager

5. to spend time in idleness _____
   a) curtail, abridge, diminish   b) abrade, chafe, graze   c) dawdle, loaf, loiter

6. to exchange views in order to arrive at the truth or to convince others _____
   a) bewilder, fluster, muddle   b) camouflage, cloak, mask   c) discuss, debate, argue

7. to relieve from constraint or restraint _____
   a) impale, lance, spear   b) laud, extol, glorify   c) unbind, liberate, emancipate

All in the Family

Select the set of related words that is the best match for the entry word below.
Write the appropriate letter in the blank.

1. prevent _____
   a) break, crack, snap   b) baffle, foil, thwart   c) appreciate, comprehend, understand

2. hesitation _____
   a) doubt, delay, reluctance   b) aid, comfort, support   c) ascent, rise, pitch

3. sloth _____
   a) apathy, listlessness, languor   b) agony, distress, misery   c) bustle, bother, flurry

4. auxiliary _____
   a) rigid, stiff, inefficient   b) likely, possible, probable   c) secondary, supplementary, subordinate

5. faithful _____
   a) loyal, steadfast, steady   b) blithe, jovial, mirthful   c) clean, fastidious, finicky

6. speech _____
   a) ardor, pep, vitality   b) ability, competence, prowess   c) articulation, voice, language

Idioms

Idioms are phrases that have meanings that are different from the overall meaning of the words that make them up. For example, the phrase *all thumbs* means "clumsy"—but if you look up the words *all* and *thumb* in the dictionary you won't find any definitions that add up to the meaning of the phrase.

If an idiom has the same meaning as the words of a synonym group, it will be included in the thesaurus entry. In Merriam-Webster thesaurus entries, idioms are listed after the synonyms and the related words.

optimistic *adj* anticipating only the best to happen and minimizing all other possibilities <was *optimistic* about book sales that year>
syn fond, Pollyannaish, sanguine, upbeat; compare HOPEFUL 1
rel bright, cheerful, merry, sunny; hopeful, hoping; assured, confident
idiom feeling on top of the world, looking on the bright side, riding (or sitting) on cloud nine

Some idioms are used in more than one form, such as *riding on cloud nine* and *sitting on cloud nine*. When this happens the thesaurus will include the variant words in parentheses. Both forms are correct and you can use whichever you like best.

One and the Same

On the bottom part of this page you will find a list of idioms and their meanings. Where would you expect to find each idiom entered in the thesaurus? Match each idiom to a word that shares its meaning in the list below. Write the number in the appropriate blank.

_____ solve   _____ compromise   _____ escape

_____ after   _____ doze   _____ boast

_____ think   _____ dance   _____ worry

_____ chatter   _____ get   _____ poor

_____ angry   _____ somehow   _____ free

_____ resemble   _____ pour   _____ fortune

1. drift off — to fall into a light sleep
2. tongue wagging — idle and often loud and incessant talk
3. king's ransom — very large amount of money
4. get to the bottom of — to find an answer or solution for (a problem or difficulty)
5. by hook or by crook — in some way not yet known or specified
6. fly the coop — to run away
7. on the house — not costing anything
8. be a dead ringer for — to be like or similar to
9. happy medium — a settlement reached by each side changing or giving up some demands
10. trip the light fantastic — to perform a rhythmic and patterned succession of steps usually to music
11. down to one's bottom dollar — lacking money or possessions
12. bite one's nails — to experience great concern
13. in the wake of — following in time or space
14. come down in buckets — to rain heavily
15. hot under the collar — feeling or showing a strong feeling of displeasure or bad temper
16. use one's head — to use one's power of reason
17. pat oneself on the back — to express pride in oneself or one's accomplishments
18. come by — gain possession of

Antonyms and Contrasted Words

In Merriam-Webster thesauruses, a word is an **antonym** when it has a basic meaning that is in direct contrast to the basic meaning of a synonym group. **Contrasted words** are words that are nearly opposite, but not quite. Often, contrasted words differ from antonyms in emphasis or in the suggestions they communicate. For example, the word *poor* is the antonym of the word *rich* because its meaning is exactly opposite and because it is similarly matter-of-fact in tone. The word *destitute* is a contrasted word. It is close to *poor* in meaning but is more emphatic (it means "very poor") and it carries a stronger suggestion of misery and distress.

In a Merriam-Webster thesaurus entry, the contrasted words and antonyms come after the synonyms, related words, and idioms. The contrasted words come before the antonyms.

ugly *adj* ...
   syn hideous, ill-favored, ill-looking, unbeautiful, uncomely, unsightly
   rel homely, plain; bizarre, grotesque; repelling, repugnant, repulsive; unattractive, uninviting, unpleasing, unprepossessing
   idiom homely as a mud (or hedge) fence, not much to look at, short on looks
   con comely, fair, good-looking, handsome, lovely, pretty; attractive, prepossessing
   ant beautiful

Find the Antonym

Select the antonym for each of the words listed below. Write the letter of the antonym in the blank.

1. absent _____
   a) adrift b) present c) dependable

2. real _____
   a) imaginary b) dreamless c) requisite

3. able _____
   a) inept b) negative c) selective

4. mirth _____
   a) fun b) sojourn c) melancholy

5. stylish _____
   a) urban b) genial c) dowdy

6. doubtful _____
   a) questionable b) indubitable c) wrong

Find the Contrasted Word

Select the word that contrasts with each of the words listed below.
Write the letter of the contrasted word in the blank.

1. downcast _____
   a) dejected b) upland c) cheerful

2. explicit _____
   a) obscure b) certain c) hydraulic

3. tyranny _____
   a) fault b) time c) freedom

4. benevolent _____
   a) beautiful b) stingy c) bewhiskered

5. persevere _____
   a) secure b) falter c) transact

6. relevant _____
   a) shy b) scared c) inappropriate

Opposites Attract

Draw lines to connect each word on the left to an antonym or contrasted word on the right.

simple	foot
selfish	correct
mature	crawl
top	complex
truth	optimist
applaud	childish
decrease	generous
pessimist	enlarge
run	dry
humid	boo
mistaken	deception

Answer Key

1. Alphabetical Order—Getting Started

Test Your Alphabet Skills
1. cat, dog, horse, mouse, pig
2. jaunt, lyric, sled, TV, umbrella
3. acrobat, lazy, noodle, octopus, vitamin

Test Your Alphabet Skills
1. bad, bike, blouse, boy, broccoli
2. seven, share, snap, store, sunny
3. icy, ignition, industry, irk, ivy

Test Your Alphabet Skills
1. chalk, cheese, chili, chop, chute
2. cannon, canopy, capable, capacious, capstan
3. draggle, dragnet, dragon, dragonfly, dragoon

2. Alphabetical Order—Moving Along

Test Your Alphabet Skills
1. figure of speech, figure out, fir, firecracker, fire escape
2. all-star, allude, any, anyone, anywise
3. double, double bass, doubleheader, double-jointed, double play
4. man, manage, management, manifold, man-made
5. signal, signboard, significance, sign language, signpost

Amazing Results!
cocoa, coconut, cocoon, doughnut, dove, granny knot, grape, grasshopper, noise, nomad, orchid, ostrich, otter, pelican, penguin, pentagon, piccolo, radish, treasure

3. Guide Words

Test Your Guide Word Skills
1. countenance, course
2. screech, scurvy
3. offensive, oily
4. merit, meteoric
5. houseboy, human
6. tan, tapestry
7. awe, baboon
8. gander, garlic
9. colorless, comet
10. cog, collection
11. sidetrack, signature
12. percussion instrument, permeating
13. sadden, sailboat
14. bare, base
15. bank, bare
16. urchin, utilization
17. human, hunter
18. huntsman, hyacinth
19. admonish, adverb
20. denuding, deputy

4. End-of-Line Divisions

Segmenting Words
1. em·per·or 2. snow·man 3. cray·on
4. ox·y·gen 5. piz·za 6. mis·con·duct
7. pa·ja·mas 8. as·ter·oid 9. ted·dy bear
10. ma·caw 11. teach·er 12. glob·al
13. zo·di·ac 14. im·per·son·al 15. pyr·a·mid
16. pick·er·el 17. platy·pus 18. obe·lisk
19. broth·er 20. re·la·tion·ship
21. ed·u·ca·tion 22. pome·gran·ate
23. im·por·tance 24. roy·al·ty 25. ori·ole
26. orang·utan 27. oc·ta·gon
28. tour·na·ment 29. mis·tle·toe 30. ko·ala

31. car·toon 32. south·west·ern
33. glock·en·spiel 34. chem·i·cal
35. atyp·i·cal 36. sand·pa·per

5. Pronunciation
What's That Sound?
1. **'**hənch 2. i-**'**käl-ə-jē
3. pər-**'**kəsh-ən 4. **'**sham-ˌräk
5. **'**zōd-ē-ˌak 6. **'**hī-bər-ˌnāt
7. fē-**'**es-tə 8. **'**yüs-fəl

What's That Word?
'ap-əl\ apple
\im-ˌaj-ə-**'**nā-shən\ imagination
'hōm-ˌwərk\ homework
'fan\ fan
'ən-yən\ onion
'fin\ fin
'jī-ənt\ giant
'hät-ˌdȯg\ hot dog
'fən\ fun
'saùth\ south
'fīn\ fine

6. More About Pronunciation
Find the Syllables
'fā-və-rə-bəl\, \ri-**'**kȯrd-ər\, **'**dī-nə-ˌsȯr\
\ə-**'**päl-ə-ˌjīz\, **'**rən-ə-ˌwā\, **'**maj-ə-stē\
'aùt-ˌpā-shənt\, \pə-**'**sif-ik\, \pə-**'**pī-ə\
'tel-ə-ˌvizh-ən\

All Stressed Out
'häl-ə-ˌdā\, **'**fül-ˌhärd-ē\, **'**mag-ˌpī\
\ˌpräb-ə-**'**bil-ət-ē\, **'**tüth-ˌbrəsh\
\ˌsed-ə-**'**ment-ə-rē\, \ˌtäp-sē-**'**tər-vē\
'wā-ˌsīd\, **'**kāt-ē-ˌdid\, \ˌnav-ə-**'**gā-shən\

Putting It All Together
'nā-vē\, **'**strȯ-ˌber-ē\, **'**tēn-ˌā-jər\
\ˌev-rē-ˌdā\, \tə-**'**lep-ə-thē\, **'**lü-mə-nəs\
\ə-**'**ləm-nə\, **'**zōd-ē-ˌak\, **'**mēt-ē-ər\
\fə-**'**nal-ē\

7. Still More About Pronunciation
Be a Dictionary Detective
'nərv-**'**fī-bər\, \ig-**'**zȯst\, \ik-**'**sting-gwish-ər\
'stȯr-mē-nəs\, \kən-**'**klü-siv-lē\
'man-ij-ər-ˌship\, **'**ī-**'**tēth\
\ˌaùt-ˌbōrd-**'**mōt-ər\, **'**fäth-fə-lē\, **'**pled\

8. Variants
Variant or Misspelling?
Cross out: capitle, barnickle, calipper, ballust, garaje, poinsetta, peddlar, sinapse, ryme, riggorous, sirrup, insentive, barel

Which Is Preferred?
Circle: hooves, judgment, smelled, fungi, shod, oxen, vacuums, quartet, juncos, eerie, encrust, shrank, hurrah, hooray, hurrah, distill, among, biceps

9. Functional Labels
Birds of a Feather
vb: go, well, remember, succeed, brief, run, cloud
n: cloud, dictionary, computer, well, scorpion, run
adj: adorable, well, our, awful, brief
adv: anywhere, strangely, well, by, but
pron: these, she, you
conj: but, or, nor, and, because
prep: beside, between, into, by, because of, but
interj: ouch, well, hello, oh, hey

10. Homographs
Which Is Which?
First column: 1, 2, 1, 3, 2
Second column: 2, 1, 4, 2, 1

Two for the Price of One
1. fall, fall 2. fans, fan 3. right, right
4. base, base 5. tense, tense 6. can, can
7. light, light 8. expressed, express
9. low, low

11. Inflected Forms
Animals and Others
mantises, mantes; knives; fungi, funguses; flamingos, flamingoes; fezzes; halves; dromedaries; quail, quails; tracheae; chassis; reindeer; geese; fish, fishes; hooves, hoofs; wolves; octopuses, octopi

It Happened One Morning
woke, saw, heard, sang, came, scared, lay, took

Good, Better, Best
2. worse, worst
3. greener, greenest
4. happier, happiest
5. wryer, wryest
6. farther or further, farthest or furthest
7. zanier, zaniest
8. windier, windiest
9. fatter, fattest
10. smaller, smallest
11. narrower, narrowest
12. muddier, muddiest

12. Usage Labels
Getting It Right
1.c, 2.b, 3.c, 4.a, 5.b, 6.c,
7.b, 8.b, 9.c, 10.a, 11.a, 12.c

13. Definitions—Meaning
Look It Up
1.b, 2.b, 3.a, 4.d

Context Is Key
1.a, 2.c, 3.b

14. Definitions—Historical Order
Tried and True
1.c, 2.a, 3.c, 4.b

Cutting Edge
1.a, 2.c, 3.b, 4.c

15. Synonyms and Cross-references
Synonyms, Synonyms
produce, regular, corridor, malted milk, effect, privately, fix, glimmer, stocky, hint, unimportant, speck

One Step, Two Step
1.a, 2.c, 3.c, 4.a, 5.b

16. Verbal Illustration
Which Phrase Fits?
1.c, 2.a, 3.b, 4.a, 5.b, 6.b

Which Meaning Matches?
1.b, 2.c, 3.b, 4.c, 5.a, 6.c

17. Usage Notes
Usual Uses
1.b, 2.d, 3.c, 4.d

Using Usage
1.a, 2.c, 3.b, 4.c

18. Undefined Entries
Words Plus
4, 16, 9, 13, 20, 14, 1, 10, 3, 8, 23, 18, 24, 21, 12, 17, 7, 5, 2, 19, 6, 22, 15, 11

19. Synonym Paragraphs
Shades of Meaning
1. joy, pleasure, enjoyment
2. repair, patch, mend
3. tranquil, calm, peaceful
4. job, task, duty

20. Phrases
Eureka!
1. put 2. blue 3. take 4. spite 5. time
6. get 7. make 8. common 9. beside
10. contrary 11. turn 12. hand
13. play 14. follow 15. spot 16. mean

What Does It Mean?
1.c, 2.a, 3.a, 4.c, 5.b, 6.c, 7.c

21. Word History Paragraphs
Where in the World?

1. Greek 2. Arabic 3. French 4. Latin
5. Old English 6. Latin 7. Greek 8. Greek
9. Czech 10. Latin 11. German 12. French
13. Arabic 14. Latin 15. German 16. Dutch
17. Italian 18. Latin 19. Old English
20. Greek

Looking Back

4, 16, 11, 5, 17, 13, 14, 15, 22, 9, 10,
7, 19, 3, 12, 2, 20, 8, 21, 6, 1, 18

22. What Is a Thesaurus?
Find The Misfit

1. tawny 2. scrawl 3. saturate 4. idolize
5. indelible 6. illumination 7. dexterous
8. rusty 9. premature 10. effectual

Dictionary Versus Thesaurus

1. yes 2. no 3. yes 4. no 5. yes 6. no
7. yes 8. yes 9. yes 10. yes

23. Meaning Cores and Verbal Illustrations
Matchmaker

5, 3, 7, 1, 4, 2, 6

Matchmaker

2, 6, 7, 1, 3, 5, 4

24. Synonyms and Related Words
Bet on a Set

1.a, 2.c, 3.b, 4.c, 5.c, 6.c, 7.c

All in The Family

1.b, 2.a, 3.a, 4.c, 5.a, 6.c

25. Idioms
One and the Same

First Column: 4, 9, 6, 13, 1, 17
Second Column: 16, 10, 12, 2, 18, 11
Third Column: 15, 5, 7, 8, 14, 3

26. Antonyms and Contrasted Words
Find the Antonym

1.b, 2.a, 3.a, 4.c, 5.c, 6.b

Find the Contrasted Word

1.c, 2.a, 3.c, 4.b, 5.b, 6.c

Opposites Attract

simple—complex
selfish—generous
mature—childish
top—foot
truth—deception
applaud—boo
decrease—enlarge
pessimist—optimist
run—crawl
humid—dry
mistaken—correct